MY PREROGATIVE
RELEASE AND FLY

The views and opinions expressed in this book are solely those of the author and do not reflect the views or opinions of Gatekeeper Press. Gatekeeper Press is not to be held responsible for and expressly disclaims responsibility for the content herein.

My Prerogative
Published by Gatekeeper Press
7853 Gunn Hwy., Suite 209
Tampa, FL 33626
www.GatekeeperPress.com

Copyright © 2024 by Keturah Hamilton
All rights reserved. Neither this book, nor any parts within it may be sold or reproduced in any form or by any electronic or mechanical means, including information storage and retrieval systems, without permission in writing from the author. The only exception is by a reviewer, who may quote short excerpts in a review.

Icons scribed by Priest Nubet

Library of Congress Control Number: 2023943848

ISBN (hardcover): 9781662937613

MY PREROGATIVE
RELEASE AND FLY

Keturah Hamilton

gatekeeper press™
Tampa, Florida

- Preface..1
- Confidence & Determination............................2
  - Prerogative...3
  - The Unicorn in You......................................4
  - My Definition of Strong Women..................5
  - Confidence is Sexy......................................6
  - Own Your Magic..7
  - You Are Not "Too Much".............................8
  - Failure..9
  - This is My Immigration Story....................10
  - Commitment...12
  - Don't Settle..14
  - Whatever Will Be, Will Be..........................15
  - You Can't Save a Drowning Man..............16
- Connection...18
  - Friendship..19
  - Smitten...22

- Texting..24
- Let's Talk Foreplay..................................26
- Ecstasy..27
- Love Letters..28
- Love & Vulnerability.................................29
  - Hopeless Romantic..............................30
  - Being Vulnerable.................................32
  - We Are Attention Seekers....................33
  - Your Type...34
  - Kissing the Frog..................................35
  - Betrayal..37
  - Wasted Time.......................................39
  - Independent Women............................40
  - Find Your Person 41
- Live and Learn.......................................42
- Jokes From My Loved Ones...................43
  - From Glad..44
- About..45
- Synopsis..46

MY PREROGATIVE

In loving memory of my dad, Fitzroy Lindsay, and my aunty Annmarie Gordon. I love you and miss you.

Keturah Hamilton

I owe it all to my Heavenly Father above for all my gifts and talents, for never giving up on me, and for His unconditional love, even when I'm not deserving of it.

Special Message

You have changed my life tremendously and poured knowledge into my vessel. Thank you both, David Tawil and Gloria Gifford.

To My Hubby

I've been around the world and back, and I never knew where I was going to land. Then, one day my entire world changed when God placed my earth angel in my life: my husband. He is my biggest cheerleader, supporter, and partner. I dedicate this book to him, because without his love, support, and guidance, this wouldn't have been possible.

My Gratitude List

To my guardian angels, I miss you all. Please continue to watch over me: Clarence Ffrench, Donald McKenzie, Howard McKenzie, Sheldon Ffrench, Nicholas McKenzie, Dean Parker, Donald Parker, Don Parker aka "Big Daddy," and the matriarch, Gladys Parker, aka "Mom."

Shout out to my friend Shay Domingo for listening to the rough draft when I first came up with the idea to write this book.

To all my loved ones: Beverly Morgan, Denzel Small—love you to the moon and back—Brittany McKenzie, Don McKenzie, Courtney McKenzie, Jr., Shadel Ffrench, Corrine Richards, Leonora Lattibeaudiere, and Saige Nesbitt.

My English tutor, Raina Kelly, who listened to me read this entire manuscript during one of our sessions. She didn't know it was a setup for her to edit it for me.

To Leslie Nesbitt, Janice Pitter, Michelle Walker, Shayla Michelle, Ewan Walker, Raven Bowens, Rusheda Clarke, Andrea Tulloch, Pablo Kennedy, Delroy Edwards, Celestina Nwokolo, Tanya Thomas, Lisa Bryan, Sabrina Won, Kamani Getfield, Damian Brown, George Winn, Corey Moses, Kamala Lane, and Virgina Scarlet. I love you all and thank you for loving me.

Preface

One night about five years ago, I randomly started writing down my thoughts. I didn't pursue this as a writer, but only to journal my emotions and experiences. I felt this urge to write about all the challenges and fears I have overcome and memories I hold near and dear. The unpredictability of the COVID pandemic really opened my eyes and put into perspective how precious life is and that it shouldn't be taken for granted.

I had honestly never considered publishing or sharing any of my deepest thoughts, until I too suffered several losses within my family. I became encouraged to live each and every day like it was my last. I felt compelled to share some of my experiences, mishaps, memorable moments, and how I learned to navigate and rise above them.

I hope when reading *My Prerogative*, you find that the passages provide you with humor, motivation, guidance, inspiration, and take you on a walk down memory lane.

Confidence & Determination

Prerogative

While writing this, I am singing the song "My Prerogative" by Bobby Brown in my head.

People are always going to have something to say no matter what. You can't allow negative criticism from others to cripple you from believing in yourself and the way you choose to live your life. You must march to the beat of your own drum and be more than just a diamond in the rough. We all have a right to be or do whatever we want, especially if our actions aren't harming another human being. Whatever mistakes I've made, I vow to take responsibility, own them, and stand firm regardless of the outcome. My choices and decisions are my prerogative and they must be respected.

The Unicorn in You

We all grow up hearing the story of the mythical creature, the unicorn. I grew up believing and living my life similar to the Jamaican saying, "Belief kills and belief cures." If you genuinely believe in the magic of life, you will believe in the unicorn within.

As a young girl, I would play dress-up and model in front of the mirror every day. I would fantasize about being on a runway with lights, cameras flickering, and the echoing of my name. I would be living the dream, falling in love, marrying a successful man.

When you are a child, many people may say that it's wishful thinking, but is it really? I know many people may judge me about wanting it all, but the unicorn in me believes that I am deserving of everything wonderful.

I am here to tell you to unleash your inner power and believe in your unique magic. Grab a pen and paper and write down why the unicorn in you is absolutely unstoppable and read it every day as a reminder to yourself.

My Definition of Strong Women

I grew up around strong, fierce, and brave women, and the strongest of them all is my mother. I witnessed my mother go through the painful experience of losing three of her sons, and, yes, it took a deep mental and emotional toll on her. She bawled her eyes out uncontrollably then, and still does to this day. She misses her sons deeply; that excruciating pain will never go away and nothing and no one can fill that void. However, throughout her suffering, her faith never wavered and she stood like the Rock of Gibraltar.

Being strong doesn't mean that you won't break into a million pieces. Strength is when you use your perseverance to pick up those pieces and live to fight another day. To all my warrior ladies, just know that we are built for this, and we're equipped for whatever life throws at us.

Love you, Mom

Keturah Hamilton

Confidence is Sexy

Sexy is beauty within! Sexy is power! Sexy is you!

Growing up, I admired and worshipped my stepdad, Clarence Ffrench, aka "Spider." I guess the saying is true, "A girl's first admiration is her dad and his teachings." I have fond memories of him praising me for how beautiful, smart, and strong I was.

That significantly helped instill confidence in myself from an early age. He taught me that I should know my worth and my value.

He would tell me, "Being beautiful is more than just my appearance," and because of him, I grew up with the mentality that beauty is about being more than a beautiful face.

Do you know beauty starts on the inside with you standing in your personal power? Stop making yourself small to fit society's standard of what is beautiful and sexy.

Be brave, be bold, and make your sexiness shine through, because confidence is what makes you sexy.

Own Your Magic

We all seek validation from others, especially from our loved ones and our friends. But is validation really necessary? Yes and no. We all have unique qualities, multiple talents, and a God-given purpose. Unfortunately, some of us run away from what makes us unique so we can fit in.

Let's rewind! When I first started modeling and participating in "go-sees," also known as auditions, it was normal to have difficulty distinguishing one model from the other because they all looked alike. That wasn't thrilling to me, because like eating the same thing every day, it can become a bit boring. We all fall into the trap of wanting to fit in and follow the trends instead of being our true, authentic self.

I was once told by someone that I am timeless, which is an amazing compliment, but I never embraced it. That is, until I realized that in order to run this marathon called life, you must remain your unique self. Your magic is what makes you different, and you will always be magical once you decide to be true to yourself.

You Are Not "Too Much"

Have you ever been labeled as "extra" or told you are "doing the most?"

I have heard these statements my entire life; and, well, they are so accurate. That's right! I refuse to dim my brightness because it makes someone feel uncomfortable. You can never be "too much." Why dim your light because others have a problem with the beautiful way you shine?

Your light is meant to be bright like the blazing sun, so be aware of everyone who is lurking in the dark. They are naysayers! They will attempt to destroy you and turn you into a bat, who never sees the light of day. Never let anyone rob you of being yourself because you weren't born to please mankind. You were born to be great and to spread love!

I admire people who never gave up, like the late Pelé, the late Kobe Bryant, Serena Williams, Usain Bolt, and Michael Jordan. In my opinion, they all have one thing in common: "being too much." They decided they wanted to be phenomenal, and they consistently shine their light without apology.

Let us all take a moment and reach beyond our expectations—because at the end of the day we are renters on Earth and will be held accountable for the legacy and the lives we touched.

Failure

What is failure? The dictionary will give you its own definition, but I don't believe in the word failure. That's just my opinion!

I believe in life lessons and timing. I am a creative person, and I have done things that have gained success and other things that didn't necessarily turn out the way I desired. Nevertheless, I didn't look at these events as a failure; they just weren't meant to happen for me at that time.

Rome wasn't built in a day, so whatever you are working on will take time and at times may seem hopeless. Unfortunately, that's when we tend to give up and label our plans as failures. To be great at anything, we must dedicate at least ten thousand hours, or ten years, to truly master that talent, no matter what career you're pursuing.

We are all so impatient. We love instant gratification so much that we give up and tell ourselves that we have failed.

Well, why don't you and I play a game? I will write out what each letter in failure means to me. Here's what I came up with. F is for Fighter. A is for Assertive. I is for Ingenuity. L is for Limitless. U is for Unwavering. R is for Resilience. E is for Excellence. Now, write what it means to you and then live it, breathe it, and believe it. Who knows? It might just be your time.

Keturah Hamilton

This is My Immigration Story

My experience leaving Jamaica was probably the equivalent of the struggle of a fish trying to survive out of water. It seemed like overnight my world turned upside down when I left my birthplace.

Back home, we say, "Yuh a go ah foreign," when someone moves to America. Leaving my third-world country for a first-world country meant moving to the "land of opportunity." However, my immigration experience was a frightening one and, let me tell you, it also came with some incredibly challenging moments. Growing up I would hear people say, "Who feels it, knows it," and, boy, did I feel it. Let me not exaggerate because I think regardless of what I went through, I did damn good for myself!

Here is my immigration story. Like most undocumented immigrants, I had to fight to become legally recognized as a member of American society. The process is extremely daunting.

When trying to gain legal validation in America, you must be careful who you trust, because your own family and friends can betray you. I learned that you must be very selective about whose help you accept, because there may come a time when you will be required to participate in an immoral or illegal act as payment for the help you received—and if you don't comply, you immediately become a victim of extortion. As selective as I was, someone I trusted still reported me to immigration enforcement out of jealousy. In their eyes I did not deserve an opportunity to climb the ladder of success. Lawd! I had never felt so afraid, hopeless, and betrayed.

My future was now in the hands of decision-makers who had the power to set my future back a thousand years. Little did I know that prayer and faith can move mountains. That's when My Heavenly Father prepared a table for me that no man could destroy. My table! And when I say, "my table," I mean it! You see, we all have something called "my time" and once it's your time, not even the serpent from hell can destroy you.

My time came, despite the dagger that was placed in my heart, when I was officially granted my US citizenship. God bless America. Life is like a disco. No matter how the music changes, just keep on dancing.

Commitment

Commitment is a very challenging thing and can be scary. It might be easy for some people to commit to something or someone and stay committed, but for others it's a life sentence. I know I can be overly dramatic, but I'm speaking from experience here.

For so long, I had a commitment issue. I felt like I would lose a part of my untamed quality because someone would be telling me when to pee, eat, or sleep—like Morgan Freeman in the movie *The Shawshank Redemption*.

Looking back on it, I had a totally different meaning in my head of what commitment truly is. Commitment can be a blessing because it can change your life in ways you didn't expect.

For me, my new perception of commitment changed how I approached life. It gave me a sense of accomplishment, like I could complete any task I started. My ability to commit allows me to see things through to the end, give it my all, and not shortchange myself. I am now able to embrace the unexpected journey of life's winding roads without the fear of giving up.

One of the worst things you can ask yourself is, "What would have happened if I had committed to following my dreams despite what other people wanted or expected of me?"

Just know this: if you commit with every fiber of your being, there is a greater chance you won't have to wonder, "What if?" To commit, you will have to lose yourself, get out of your own way, and leave your comfort zone.

Don't Settle

Children tend to mirror what they see growing up, especially if they witness abusive relationships. Whether the abuse is physical, mental, or emotional, parents will sometimes stay in that relationship even though it's not what's best for their kids. The children who witness these abusive relationships may believe that such behavior is part of life and settle for the same in their own lives. Sometimes it's hard to unlearn what was instilled in us. Facing your past can either make you stronger or destroy you.

I am so proud of one of my besties who survived the foster system and sexual abuse and turned it into a positive trajectory for her life. Given her circumstances, she could have played the victim. She could have let fear and torment destroy her entire future. Instead, she chose courage and became the woman she knew she was meant to be: strong, beautiful, capable, and worthy. Like a boxer who was just knocked down, you can either push through and get up, or allow your opponent to win. I am not saying it's easy, but you need to decide if you are going to roll over and play dead or stand up and fight. My friend got up like the champion she was born to be, decided to overcome her past, and said, "I will not be defeated."

Now that's a badass.

Whatever Will Be, Will Be

I am a strong believer in whatever will be, will be. If we live by this philosophy, we can significantly decrease the stress we deal with on a daily basis. I had a dear friend that I admired and relied on. One time, I did something that she perceived as selfish and unfortunately, we got into a heated argument. She told me that I was going to fall off the high horse I was riding on. She felt that I was acting like I was better than everyone else and that my life wouldn't be a success. Although I found her words to be hurtful and vindictive, my belief is it doesn't matter what another person wishes for your life. Your story and your destiny are already written. Nobody can stop what's ordained for us, and no one can predict whether someone else's life will be smooth sailing or not. Just know that whatever will be, will be. Whatever is meant for you can never be taken away from you and no one can foresee your future.

You Can't Save a Drowning Man

I was raised to love, to be kind, and to share.

My stepdad was a selfless man. I remember when he would cook for our entire community every Friday and help families with children in need. That's the kind of generosity I saw growing up. So, I live my life with the idea of "loving and being kind."

What I didn't realize is that some people will take advantage of your kindness and drag you down with them.

Your surroundings can include two types of people: the good and the parasites. A parasite's mentality is that the world owes them something. Maybe this is because the people they thought they could count on screwed them over. Maybe they feel misunderstood and need a break. It's easy to get so caught up in their pity party that you start sacrificing your entire being. The parasites will take everything you have and keep coming back for more until you are completely exhausted and drained of whatever resources they wanted. Once you tell the parasites, "No more!"—they will turn on you, read you the riot act, and try to make you feel like you're at the bottom of the barrel. Don't give in to their ramblings. You must stand your ground because the worst thing that you can do is become an enabler; that would be a disservice to you.

MY PREROGATIVE

Ask yourself this question: when you're on a plane and the oxygen masks drop, why do you think it's important to put on your mask first before helping others? When you see someone drowning, why are we advised not to rescue them by jumping in? For you to be able to save someone else you must first take care of yourself. And like a parasite, a distressed or panicked swimmer will put you in danger as they attempt to use you as a flotation device to save themselves. Unfortunately, some people have learned the hard way that you can't save a drowning man.

Connection

Friendship

Friendships can be challenging and should be treated like a committed relationship. It's imperative that you put time and effort into making sure your friends know that you care for, love, and cherish them. Oh boy, but sometimes you mess up big time.

I grew up as the only girl in my family with three brothers. I sure do love them, but I always wondered what it would have been like to have a sister to argue with, steal my clothes, share my deepest, darkest secrets with, and, most importantly, to love.

Unfortunately, that didn't happen, so I had to embrace my girlfriends as my sisters. Sometimes it was bittersweet because I naïvely held onto some fake friendships for too long because I wanted a sister so badly.

However, I have been blessed with wonderful, loyal, and loving friends.

My friend Janice is my big sister. She's as crazy as they come, but our friendship is like the wedding vow "for better or worse." You can't help but love her, but you also have to prepare for that storm.

Leslie is my smooth, levelheaded friend, and we speak the same language. We are go-getters and we take no prisoners.

Ewan is a puzzle that you are always trying to figure out. Some days you might get it right and other days you won't, but I know we'll be friends to the end, like Chucky.

These three friends are so completely different, but all have one thing in common: they are my oldest and dearest friends, and they respect and love me in their own way. Don't get me wrong, I'm not saying that we don't cuss each other out. Oh, we have major disagreements, but what friendships don't? Sometimes we go years without speaking, but through it all we always come back together.

I remember when Ewan, Leslie, and I would count our quarters so we could eat. We've cried together; we've gotten in trouble together; we've laughed together; and we were never afraid to tell one another to shove it where the "sun don't shine." These are real relationships. It takes years of understanding, commitment, love, and dedication to keep these friendships going.

Friends will come and go, but memories will always remind you that you must cherish the moments you shared, good or bad. You will even make new friends along the way.

Just know that you will have to start the process all over again. You'll need to build trust, make memories, and hope that the relationship will last a lifetime instead of becoming a distant memory. Like any relationship, a friendship can be destroyed like shattered glass and never be repaired.

Nevertheless, I strongly believe in the saying, "Good friends are worth more than money in the bank."

Smitten

The first time I laid eyes on him, I felt like my entire existence was out of control. I couldn't eat, I couldn't speak, I couldn't sleep; I felt like my stomach was tied up into knots. My heart was beating so fast; I thought something was seriously wrong with me. All I could see was him, constantly, in everything I did.

It was so scary because I didn't think it was normal for a young girl to have such deep feelings for a boy. I would constantly hear his voice in my ears. His voice was the sweetest I'd ever heard, and his smile was so inviting. It made me feel safe and loved. What did I know about love? I knew my parents loved me, but was that the same thing?

Mikey James, that was his name! He was a popular track star, and he was fine as hell. I often found myself daydreaming that one day I would take his last name. I would write our names a hundred times with hearts all over the paper and listen to love songs all day long. I felt like I was losing my mind and I would end up in an insane asylum for having all these uncontrollable feelings. Eventually, he told me that he also wrote my name all day long and I was the first and the last person he thought about every day.

I just remember thinking, "LAWD, please." I couldn't handle hearing all of this. I was going to live happily ever after. The stars in my heart were flickering so hard,

MY PREROGATIVE

I was surprised I didn't catch on fire. No, we weren't having sex, but we would show affection by kissing and buying each other chocolates and postcards. We were inseparable and super popular among our friends. You wouldn't see us apart. We would dress alike and even started to look alike. I know it sounds funny but, truth be told, when you are young and in love, no one can tell you anything. The more my aunty Dimples would forbid me from seeing him, the more I became a smitten kitten.

I grew up as an Adventist, so I know a thing or two about the Bible and its many stories. So, like Eve, I wanted that forbidden fruit so badly, no matter what. It's not easy to be a young girl because you will experience the craving to know it all. However, it's impossible to know it all when you have never lived.

At the time, I didn't want my elders to correct me because in my "extensive, worldly" experience, I believed that it was my life and, regardless of the unsolicited advice I received, I was going to do as I pleased. Yes, as a young girl, I felt like I knew everything. I remember my aunty saying, "Don't rush to grow up. Enjoy your youth because being an adult sucks." Yeah right, what does she know? Well, with age comes wisdom, and the longer you live the more you experience. The lesson I learned was that your high school love may or may not be your soul mate. This was a lesson that I learned the hard way.

Texting

At some point in time, we've all blown a gasket because we took something someone said out of context. Especially in today's world, where we don't pick up our phone or have face-to-face conversations. Instead, we simply text.

People text or email everything, even to break up with someone who they planned to spend the rest of their life with. Sadly, texting is a convenient way to avoid human connection.

I am guilty of being an active member of the texting world. I love to hear my phone ring as opposed to hearing a text notification and, when I look at my phone, a message pops up.

"Baby, I love you."

For a moment that might be cute, but is it satisfying? You can't hear the emotion and passion of a human voice through a text message. I remember receiving a text message once that I completely misunderstood, and it ruined a budding relationship with a potential love interest before the relationship really had a chance to bloom.

MY PREROGATIVE

Texting is great when you don't want to be bothered with someone because that's the easiest way to avoid and dismiss them! Call me pathetic, but I miss the days when I would fall asleep on the phone with my new crush, who couldn't get enough of me. When I saw that he was calling me, my heart would skip a beat. That's my love language.

Let's Talk Foreplay

Everyone has a different interpretation of the word foreplay. Foreplay is the ultimate beginning of sex, and emotional and physical intimacy.

However, when it comes to me, I say, "Forget about the foreplay. Let's just get down to the nitty gritty."

That's how bad I want it, but is that true? Am I just running from the emotion and the intimacy of wanting to connect? Why can't I connect on a deeper level? The good girl in me wants every inch of my body to be loved. I want to experience the gentleness of his touch, the taste of his lips, the warmth of his breath, and the feel of his body pressing against mine. What a feeling of euphoria.

Don't be embarrassed by what intoxicates you. Your secret is safe with me.

Ecstasy

He stood there and stared at me with those big, beautiful eyes. I started to get butterflies fluttering in my stomach. My entire body began to get wet like a broken faucet, and I knew then and there that I was addicted.

The touch of his hand running all over my body, the smell of his breath, the way he groaned like a lion coming out of his cage, and the poetry he spoke. The way he laid me down and called my name. The way he ravished my nakedness. We would lie there quietly, breathing on each other and staring into each other's eyes, wondering what made us so sexually drawn to each other. My inner voice was saying, "Girl, it's those lips and beautiful eyes." Another voice was saying, "Face the truth! It's the sexual ecstasy!"

Once it was time for him to go, I felt empty again. It was as if a drug I just took wore out of my system. It's easy to convince yourself that you are in control because you don't want to admit that you have an addiction. Even if I could have accepted it, the truth is that I didn't want to be cured.

Love Letters

I have a box of love letters stored away. There's something sexy about a man who writes to a woman. There's something to be said about the butterflies you feel in your stomach while reading that letter—the twinkle in your eyes and the smile plastered all over your face, not to mention that your heart is laughing.

Some love letters are so eloquently written that you'd think it was William Shakespeare writing to you.

That memory of love letters reminds me of the story when Don, my father-in-law, started courting my mother-in-law, Glad. When he left for the army, she told him she would wait for him. While at war, he wrote her love letters, and that was her assurance that once he was back, they would get married and bear children.

I love movies like *The Patriot*, where the late Heath Ledger's character, Gabriel, goes off to war and communicates through letters to the young woman he was planning to marry.

I am a sucker for true love, and a lover of love letters.

Love & Vulnerability

Hopeless Romantic

Have you ever loved somebody so much it makes you cry?

Love is a roller coaster, and you must be willing to take that ride knowing that, at any moment, it might come to an end. Your head and your heart may be left in pieces.

Oh boy! What a feeling! It's like the roller coaster didn't just take you for a wild ride, but it took you on a journey where aliens ate you up. No matter how much your heart is beating, and you are holding on for dear life, the more you fight, the more likely the roller coaster will knock you around.

While one voice in your head is telling you, "Fight, because it's worth it!"; the other voice is saying, "Love shouldn't hurt, so why are you putting up with this?"

Well, love does hurt and, yes, the pain runs deep. But what is life without getting on that roller coaster? Even if it's only for a day? Think about it. The late Elizabeth Taylor, Jennifer Lopez, Pamela Anderson, and many others were married multiple times and found happiness each time. I guess the saying is true, "What's life without experiencing love?"

Let go, brush it off, get back on, and take that ride. You never know what the future holds. If it's not going in your direction, get off and get on another ride, and another one, until things are going in your direction.

It's okay to not know where the roller coaster will take you, but it might just be the right ride and you might enjoy it for the rest of your life . . . or not! Are you afraid of getting on a roller coaster? Well, most of us are, so it's time to break that fear.

Being Vulnerable

My acting teacher stresses the importance of yearning and being vulnerable. If you are an actor, you must possess the right skills to show these two elements in your work.

To be vulnerable and yearn aren't easy things to do. We are all humans with all sorts of baggage and scars. Over the years we learn to protect ourselves with a shield, but that shield becomes heavy. It gets lost or buried so deeply that it may be difficult to find.

So, we guard our hearts and our thoughts so much so that we tend to forget how to show vulnerability. No, vulnerability is not a sign of weakness, but a sign of the humanness of being physically or emotionally wounded, especially by the people we love and trust.

Women should be strong, fierce, and independent. However, when it's time to yearn and be vulnerable, we need to open our heart chakra. The heart chakra serves as our center of love for oneself and others. Allow yourself to experience the freedom of letting down your walls and getting in touch with your vulnerability.

We Are Attention Seekers

What's wrong with a girl wanting some attention? We all have a childlike quality in us, no matter how old we are. Sometimes we throw a temper tantrum and act like a toddler wanting a lollipop.

Most of us are emotional beings, especially when we can't get what we want! Women are delicate flowers, but we don't want to be treated like something that's weak or to be pitied.

We just need to be treated with love, affection, admiration, and a whole lot of attention. Yes, I said it! We want to be attended to and feel like we belong to the person we love.

Isn't that just a part of what makes us women?

Your Type

Are you often asked, "What's your type?"

Some responses may be, "Dark, tall, muscular, short, rich, educated, Caucasian, Spanish, Puerto Rican, Jamaican, British, European," and the list goes on.

A "type" is mainly an appearance that we visualize in our heads; then we get stuck and can't let go of that fantasy. Don't get me wrong, sometimes your image becomes your Prince Charming or your dream girl. I was once asked specifically, 'What's your type?' and I thought about it carefully before answering, "A man with a good heart, who loves and respects his mother."

We all want to be with someone who complements us, and with whom we have something in common. However, the truth of the matter is that sometimes who we want isn't good for us, and the person we think is too soft, simple, or "not our type" may be the person who will move mountains for us, water our seeds, and save us from going down like the *Titanic*.

Just don't be set on your type. Trust his heart and give that man a chance!

Kissing the Frog

Have you ever asked yourself, while laughing uncontrollably, "What was I thinking when I dated that guy back then? Was I going through something? Is something wrong with me?"

Well, let's rewind back to when that guy—we'll call him "Peter"—claimed not only did we date, but we slept together.

I asked him, "Slept together? When and where?"

"You don't remember?" he said nonchalantly.

"No, I don't remember, so please refresh my memory! You know what? Don't!" I said defensively.

The voice inside my head said, "It must have been so horrible that I blocked it out and now have no recollection of that night, or of him."

We definitely go through stages, regrets, and moments that we would do anything for a do-over. The funny thing about life, though, is that we can't erase what's been done. We can only move forward. Hopefully, we will learn and grow from what we once thought was a mistake or a screwup.

You can look at it as an adventure, cry about it, or hold yourself accountable, but never forget to smile through it because it's a good chapter in the story of your life.

Who wants to read a boring book? Chin up, ladies! Just remember, we've all kissed a frog somewhere down the road. We are all in this together!

Betrayal

We all know the story of Samson and Delilah. It's considered a "romantic" biblical drama. We have all written, starred, directed, and acted out our own romantic drama at some point in our lives. Although Samson, a faithful servant, was mesmerized by this beautiful woman, Delilah, sometimes the tables flip, and a woman gets mesmerized by a "Samson." So, women aren't the only seducers; men are seducers also. Have you ever had someone betray you in the name of love or for some other hidden agenda? I have been betrayed so many times, and if I am being honest, I have done my fair share of betraying.

Betrayal is never easy. It can break us into a million different pieces and have us curled up in an emotional ball. I have experienced betrayal to the extent that I thought I would never recover. Have you ever felt pain so deeply that it was like a knife being pushed through your heart—and just when you thought it was done, it just kept twisting? I didn't expect to experience so much pain because I thought my ex and I were unbreakable. We shared six years together, and I thought he was "the one" because I had never experienced love like that before. He was tender, protective, supportive, unique, and showed me that love does exist.

What went wrong? Well, I am not sure, but I might have played a role in the web of deceit. I do know one thing for sure: he was put in my life for a reason, to teach me a very valuable lesson. If I could do it all over again, I wouldn't change a thing. Am I a fool? No, heartbreak is a part of life. Did it hurt? Yes, of course. Just know that everything—good or bad—happens for a reason, and in the moment, you might not understand because you are in so much pain.

There is always a light at the end of the tunnel. If you hold on long enough, someone magical may be waiting for you. Sometimes, you must go through the burning fire to meet "Mr. Unforgettable," who will take you to a much higher level. To move forward, you must be willing to mentally and emotionally remove bitterness and revenge.

It's not easy, but ask yourself, "Do I walk around beating myself up?" Do you think, "All men are the same?" You can't know unless you try, and it will take work and time.

Experience is our teacher, and regrets and blame are like a death sentence. Hold on to hope and don't let go; not everyone is a "Delilah."

Wasted Time

Time is so precious and yet we waste it every single day of our lives, whether on things or people. It's as if we forget that we can't rewind the clock. Once it's gone, we can't get it back.

I know at one point in my life, I didn't understand the importance of time. If I did, I wouldn't have spent years chasing after friends, ex-boyfriends, and things that weren't putting me on a path to becoming a better me. Ladies, have you ever wasted time or energy on a man who wasn't worthy of you?

When you allow time-suckers to monopolize your time, it's easy to overlook how quickly those minutes can turn into years. I know women who have spent decades hoping their love could change a man, sticking around and keeping up the facade of being with somebody, just because they fear feeling stupid. They were probably warned and still pursued the relationship or friendship, not realizing that they were wasting time, energy, and effort.

Don't get me wrong; not all relationships are hopeless, but no one can change a person—or force a person to respect or value them or their time.

So be brave enough to say goodbye. Life will reward you with a new you.

Independent Women

Most women love the phrase "I am independent." Like the soldiers and warriors, most women wear this as armor to protect themselves and prove that they can do it all without the help of a man or anyone who offers to help.

Being independent is good and liberating. However, to what extent should a woman be independent? Some women tend to compete with men and may lose sight of what makes us women, which is our femininity.

Allowing yourself to be cared for by a good man shouldn't take away from your independence—
but enhance your independence and partnership. Knowing you have a good partner next to you to uplift, motivate, and cheer you on is not a bad thing. I get it; women are strong and can move mountains, but being strong doesn't mean we need to lose who we are by becoming rigid and hard.

Ladies, we deserve everything wonderful, so let's not allow our drive for liberation to dictate our narrative. Let go and let that man rub those feet. You deserve it!

Find Your Person

Ladies, you are phenomenal and priceless and should be treated with love, just like back in the days when gentlemen were true gentlemen.

Glad and Don were married for sixty-four years and shared a whirlwind of experiences, all while having babies. When Glad was asked how she managed to have children back-to-back, her response was, "I was hard of hearing. Well, every night before bed Don would ask me, 'Do you want to go to sleep or what?' I'd say, 'What!'"

The proof is in the pudding; they conceived twelve children! Glad proclaimed that Don is the only man she has ever been with in her entire life, which wasn't unusual back in those days. It had to be that way. In today's world, we don't play by those rules, at least not all of us!

We can all have a "Don" in our lives if we know our self-worth. You can teach someone how to treat you, but if they don't want to play ball, you need to get a different goalkeeper. You can also hang in there and hope your love can change him or her. But unfortunately, nine out of ten times it never does; don't get discouraged because you never know! You can find your Don!

Live and Learn

I hope after taking this journey with me you can take a moment to exhale, knowing that you aren't alone and that, no matter who we are, we all face life's challenges every day.

My darling friend went through the most devastating loss of her life. Through her quest for answers and healing, she met Pope Francis. His advice to her was to strengthen her relationship with God, have faith, and surrender. All you have to do is just "show up" and He will prevail.

Remember, nothing lasts forever but the good salvation. Tomorrow will be a brighter day and bring a brighter you. Keep on climbing! The top of the mountain is closer than you think!

Love you all,

Keturah Hamilton

Jokes from My Loved Ones

From "Big Daddy" Don Parker:

Two young nuns who recently graduated from college were told by Mother Superior that they were refurbishing the convent. She asked them to paint the interior, and they quickly accepted. When the two young nuns began the job, they realized the white paint would stain their black habits. One nun suggested that since they were the only ones there, they should take off their habits and paint naked. The other agreed, so they did, and began painting. After an hour or so, they heard a knock at the door. They looked at each other in shock. Then they heard the knock again and a man yelled, "Blind Man!" The nuns looked at each other and one said, "If he's blind, there's no harm in letting him in." The other nun agreed. When they opened the door, the man said, "Nice tits, sisters! Where do you want me to hang these blinds?"

From Glad:

I childproofed my house, but they still get in.

A guy was sitting on a bench with a lady, and he said to her, "Do you believe in the hereafter?" She said, "Yes." And he replied, "Do you know what I am here after?"

A man asked his mother, "Did you clean up the mess around the house?" And his mom replied, "I told you not to marry her!"

About

Keturah Hamilton is an actress, model, and humanitarian from Jamaica, West Indies. She lives in Los Angeles.

Find Keturah on
Instagram and Facebook: @KeturahHamilton.

Synopsis

A reflection, a reassurance, and a love letter to the self, *My Prerogative: Release and Fly* explores love, heartbreak, friendship, and vulnerability. Honest, direct, and raw, author Keturah Hamilton's perseverance over life's obstacles promises to positively impact any reader in need of a powerful pick-me-up. *My Prerogative* is inspiration to the authentic self, fueling determination to thrive no matter what unpredictability life may bring.